D1608829

The Reposed

The Reposed

PHOTOGRAPHS BY WILLIAM K. GREINER

FOREWORD BY THOMAS LYNCH

INTRODUCTION BY STEVEN MAKLANSKY

LOUISIANA STATE UNIVERSITY PRESS

BATON ROUGE

To my friend, benefactor, and grandmother
Leah Bell Kross

Photographs copyright © 1999 by William K. Greiner
Text copyright © 1999 by Louisiana State University Press
All rights reserved
Manufactured in Hong Kong through Phoenix Offset
First printing
08   07   06   05   04   03   02   01   00   99
5   4   3   2   1

Designer: Laura Roubique Gleason
Typeface: ITC Galliard

Library of Congress Cataloging-in-Publication Data:
Greiner, William K.
    The reposed / photographs by William K. Greiner ; foreword by
Thomas Lynch ; introduction by Steven Maklansky.
        p.   cm.
    Greiner, William K.
    ISBN 0-8071-2413-3 (cloth : alk. paper)
    1. Photography, Artistic.   2. Cemeteries—Louisiana Pictorial
works.   I. Title.
TR654.G743   1999
779'.93931—dc21   99-26453
                                                              CIP

The paper in this book meets the guidelines for permanence
and durability of the Committee on Production Guidelines for Book
Longevity of the Council on Library Resources. ∞

FOREWORD

BY THOMAS LYNCH

The burial of the dead, like the birthing of babies, inclines us toward the existential voids. At the edges of this life, the questions are still childlike: where do we come from, where are we going, how long till we get there, have we lost our way? Whether the grave is the end or a beginning, it is certainly a stop; whether destination point or port of call, all down the history of the species we have marked the spot and in those markings sought to say that the buried dead beneath them mattered, in a variety of ways, and the space assigned to them ought not be tampered with.

Indeed, first among the signs of civilizing impulses found in the ancient landscape were the graves. Before we found the killing tools and kitchenwares and bones, we found the cairns, dolmens—those deliberate heaps of stones that said our kind was here before. We buried our dead before we discovered alphabets or farming. At first the impulse was, no doubt, olfactory. The urge to dispose of the dead was practical—they smelled bad, didn't work, and were troublesome in other ways. It soon became clear something would have to be done. But to do so by ceremony and ritual and deed bespoke an evolving sense that something more was needed here. And the marking of the spot followed as the subtle notions of memory and a Maker and an afterlife made noises in the collective mind of man. The relationship between bodies in motion and at rest, the quick and the dead, the former and present and future tense, informed this ancient

and honorable agreement that we witness and keep track of our own. Not because it matters to the dead, but because the dead matter to the living in ways best articulated in the terrible stillness of stone.

A thousand years before the pyramids were built, a society otherwise unknown to us spent three or four generations building the white quartz mortuary mound at Newgrange north of Dublin. The stone they used was not local. Boats were built to bring huge boulders north, up from Wicklow by the Irish Sea and up the River Boyne, then uphill to the point that overlooked the valley. A cave was hollowed out of the hillside, a tunnel dug into the round interior. There the dead were burned, their bones stored in stone bowls and jars in surrounding chambers. This singular enterprise required visionary leadership, personnel management, a division of labor. Hunters, gatherers, planters and harvesters, cooks and caretakers, boatsmen, haulers and high priests—all the makings of a civilization were engaged to build a kind of city of the dead. And five thousand years later, what is left are the stones.

The white face of the mound can be seen for miles through the Irish mist—a monument to the makers' vision and muscular will. And as testimony of their vast intelligence, a portal in the stoneface was built that lets the light in one day a year to illuminate the inner chamber on the winter solstice. Such deliberate stones are found all around the planet—the effort of mortals to put on immortality.

In each of our lives there are the graves of the dead. I remember being startled in Atlanta on Auburn Avenue beside Ebenezer Baptist Church to see the island tomb of Dr. Martin Luther King, Jr. It floats—a vessel of white marble—in a blue reflecting pool beside the church he and his father and his mother's father preached in. Across the street the new church is being built. Life goes on. The traffic comes and goes. But between the eternal flame and the great tomb of the great man, life is still and hushed and the pilgrim may reflect on the name and numbers cut in stone: The Reverend Dr. Martin Luther King, Jr. 1929–1968. Godhelpus, he was not yet forty! A father, a husband, a martyred man, killed for a cause he believed in with such passion that he convinced a nation to believe in it as well. And the great incantation from his own speech—Free at last, free at last, thank God Almighty I'm free at last—it is there, cut in stone, for all to see.

And I remember the rows of numbered but otherwise nameless dead at Gettysburg and the monuments around the battlefield there and elsewhere around the globe where flags and causes and crowns were fought over.

Or the eternal flame at Arlington where Irish moss and Irish stones mark the grave of Kennedy, killed too young in my youth, early in that lethal decade. We come to see what's there: his widow, his baby son, and down the hill his brother, another casualty in a century of killings.

And I think of the pilgrimages I've made to the graves of W. B. Yeats in Sligo and James Dean in Indiana and Karl Marx in Highgate Cemetery in London and all the other famous men and famous women. How the grave told me something about them and about the memory of them.

Or the island grave at Althorp where Princess Diana's body is and how the British worry over it becoming a kind of Graceland—the fashions change but the fundamentals, the marking and the memorialization do not change.

Or the graves in Holy Sepulchre at home, where my father and my mother are buried beneath a Celtic cross in which is cut "Love One Another" because it sounds like them: the moment caught, all of this life's verbs slowed to a standstill, where a stone holds forth against the busy movement of mean time.

The dead and the living require witnesses—some testimony to the fact of their being. The marked graves of the dead provide such witness. The efforts of the living to keep track and to distinguish their dearly gone but not forgotten from the general population of the cemetery seem at once both noble and futile. The grave speaks volumes and keeps silent all the same. And the images that William Greiner gives us in this exquisite collection serve, likewise, as witness to the odd confluence of the mundane and extraordinary, the corruptible and the incorruptible that marks the spot of The Reposed.

Eventually they endear us to those of our kind to whom the dull math of mortality—we all die—is not enough. They seek some meaning beyond the grim equations, beyond the black-and-white calculus of being and ceasing to be. To the stark realities Greiner's startling camera brings the full color, richly textured, deftly focused truth of the matter that there are other mysteries to behold. Who left this pink bicycle beside the tombs, upturned, balanced on its seat and turquoise handlebars? Or what are these poor florals trying to say? A Styrofoam oval wrapped in pink ribbon atop a bouquet of rotting flowers, all of it impaled on a green wire easel oddly humanoid, oddly animate beside a nameless lawn crypt in a yard of cement vaults? When does the Madonna sleep that stands atop this mausoleum? Where's the meaning in these storm clouds gathering over Einstein's family plot? Why is it that, as the notice board in New Orleans instructs us, ALL GRAVES MUST BE KEPT CLEAN ALL YEAR ROUND?

How best to remember the names and dates? These adverbials, when answered, become only reportage. But when posed, as Greiner poses them, between image and imagination, they achieve that risky balance we assign to art. If God is in the details, what's in these arti-facts and artificials? Floral Bibles and Baby Jesuses, plastic crucifixions, ceramic fish, stuffed bears and bingo boards, red rocks, blue carnations, broken hearts and Harley Davidsons—the detail and debris, left-overs among the mortal remains—does the camera tell us something or show us something? And why this manifest appreciation of shadow and vivid color, store-bought memorials and blue horizons; this fas-cination with fences, wrought iron and rough board and chain-link? Do the dead keep to their borders? Do they have unfinished business? Do they do it at Dollar or Winn-Dixie stores?

From his travels throughout Louisiana, Greiner returns laden with local and larger wisdoms. If not exactly answers, he brings back ques-tions better formed. A breakable ceramic dog keeping guard on a Barre granite monument in Gonzales, a red-and-white heart on the fresh clay in Kentwood, a teddy bear between tombs in Robert, a bas-ket of plastic flowers hung on a fence in Bogalusa—these objects punctuate the common speech of loss and precious memory, wonder and wishful thinking, faith and faith's shadows of doubt: despair and fear. They articulate the singularly human hope, in the face of all the evidence to the contrary, in a life beyond this life, in the possibility that the dead know the hearts of the living, that the last word belongs not to death but to life. His camera isolates the metaphors and icons of decay, renewal, permanent affection, endless love. He locates the odd juxtapositions, random proximities, deliberate installations, avail-able light and enhanced visions that are common to the cities of the dead. And in doing so he bears witness to the best of our instincts. His photographs hold forth in the oxymoronic idioms of still life—like bowls of fruit on a table, these dead flowers assembled on white tombs between blue skies and greensward are islands in a sea of per-petual motion where time heals, God is good, life goes on, and the dead are everywhere. His images provide new icons, sacred, secular, and silly, by which we glimpse the organizing principles of grief and good riddance. The pallet ranges between the sublime and the ridicu-lous and in doing so provides a narrative of late-century life and death and commemorative detail.

The sense it makes, like any terrible beauty, resides in the traffic Greiner willingly steps out into, sometimes busy, sometimes lonely, between the eye of the camera and beholder. He beckons us to fol-low—and, on the strength of this remarkable work, we do.

Excavating *The Reposed*

Digging Up the Meaning of Photographs by William Greiner

by Steven Maklansky

What was William Greiner getting at when he decided to title this series of photographs *The Reposed*? Was he simply describing the people who don't appear in his pictures—the buried, the entombed—and expressing our trust that in their deaths they are truly at rest and have achieved the tranquillity implied by the word *reposed*? Or does the title also refer to what people do in front of the camera when they are alive, and how their wills, their loved ones, their morticians, their graves, their cemeteries, their visitors, or even an interloping photographer will *re*-pose them in death? Either way, these photographs are not just of places: they are portraits. Although nobody appears in them, William Greiner's images still describe a colorful cast of characters, alive and dead, whose traces he finds in some of the cemeteries of New Orleans and southern Louisiana.

An intersection of cultural influences, religious doctrines, architectural styles, economic realities, municipal zoning proclamations, geological formations, and simply the passage of time has made these graveyards unusual, lugubrious, and photogenic. The most obvious distinction of south Louisiana's cemeteries is that, in many of them, hardly anyone is actually buried. Here in the delta where the Mississippi meets the Gulf of Mexico, the land is flat, wet, and often below sea level. Digging a coffin-size ditch in these swamplike conditions creates something that looks like a muddy swimming pool, good for a crawfish but bad for a corpse. Instead, coffins are placed in elevated tombs, vaults, and mausoleums. The architecture of these crypts is as eclectic and diversified as the immigrant populations that settled here and replicates the older cemeteries of the Europe from whence they came.[1] Truly cities of the dead, New Orleans's cemeteries contain stone or brick buildings, marble statues, wrought-iron fences, major arteries, narrow passages, and hidden enclaves. And like any city, they are densely packed with bodies.

The disposal of the dead is primarily an emotional challenge for the bereaved, but if it is not kept up with, it can become a significant municipal problem as well. This was especially true in nineteenth-century New Orleans, when the combination of such factors as a rapidly growing population, periodic and devastating yellow fever epidemics, and naive medical care created standing-room-only conditions in the city's old cemeteries. More typical American graveyards look and feel less metropolitan. With far fewer structures and far more stone slabs, they seem more agrarian—vast fields of gray and petrified crops.

By the second half of the nineteenth century, New Orleans's old cemeteries, already bearing signs of age and wear as handsome metaphors of human mortality, were appreciated not only as sites for internment and mourning, but as sights to see. Morbid and romantic in ways best appreciated by a Victorian sensibility, these graveyards no longer held many funerals (they were full) and catered to fewer

the hundreds of gift shops in the French Quarter; you are sure to find images of cemeteries, good for placing in a scrapbook, mailing to a friend, or confirming that New Orleans looks as it is advertised.

When Kodak introduced its first camera in 1888 with the slogan "You press the button, we do the rest," the amateur photography boom commenced. Instead of buying someone else's photographs of a famous place, you could now author your own. Just as photography had initially helped to create and then to satisfy the public's desire to see pictures from around the globe, the medium soon expanded to both encourage and justify the public's eagerness to travel. Of course, other technological advances occurring during roughly the same era (consider the light bulb, the telephone, and the affordable automobile) also fueled consumers' nomadic impulses. But the photographic empowerment of the common man and woman enabled them to record their journeys with gratifying authenticity.

St. Louis No. 1. Edward L. Wilson, 1884
New Orleans Museum of Art: Gift of the Adirondack Museum. Acc. no. 76.256.73

true mourners (as years pass, so does the normal frequency of graveside vigils). Instead, casual visitors came to look, and so did a more dedicated and better-equipped type of tourist: the photographer.

Although much of their business was in portraiture, local photographers of the era, such as Theodore Lilienthal, Samuel T. Blessing, and George F. Mugnier, also produced scenic views. Their photographs of cemeteries—as well as other attractions specific to New Orleans, such as its riverboats, expansive antebellum estates, and Jackson Square—were marketed to New Orleanians and to the curious eyes and minds of both national and international consumers. These photographs (and some quite similar images produced and sold by the thousands by large stereoview manufacturers such as Underwood and Underwood and Keystone View that thrived from approximately 1870 to 1920) assisted in creating a common and enduring visual iconography for the Crescent City. Today the existence of such visual clichés is easily confirmed by looking through the postcard racks in

New Orleans Cemetery. Grant L. Robertson, 1993
Courtesy of the photographer

Not surprisingly, many camera-toting tourists continue to document their visits to local cemeteries. Often pointing their lenses at the crypts of politicians and celebrities, and at other highlights mapped in their guidebooks or selected by their tour guides, these visitors take snapshots that, with luck, will look just like postcards. Their amateur efforts record what it was they saw, and additionally will serve as proof to their friends, families, and even their own memories that they really did see it with their own eyes. Taking pictures is thus a modern and noninvasive method of marking the boundaries of one's territory. Instead of leaving your scent or some graffiti that memorializes your presence (I was here), you make a photograph of a place to savor sometime in the future as an elapsed experience (I was there). Another significant characteristic of amateur tourist photographs is that they all look pretty much alike.

The aspiration to distinguish one's photographs from those produced by the masses has been one of the driving forces behind the development of what is now considered "artistic" photography. In addition to the thousands and thousands of dull photographers who are satisfied if their photographs of local cemeteries merely look like everyone else's, there have also been skilled and sensitive practitioners—let's call them artists—who show us that there are unique ways of seeing even the most familiar subjects, ways we would be blind to, were it not for their endeavors.

Edward Weston came to New Orleans in 1941 and took pictures in many of the city's cemeteries. At age fifty-five he was one of the country's most prominent photographers. His work was shown in books and magazines, galleries and museums, and four years earlier he had become the first photographer to receive a Guggenheim Foundation Fellowship. During the long and steady course of his artistic development he had eschewed the painterly style of pictorialist photography that was popular during the first decades of the twentieth

century and instead played a seminal role in leading a generation of photographers to a more singularly photographic aesthetic. By mastering the unique capabilities of his chosen equipment and medium (a large-format camera and the gelatin silver print), Weston felt that he could aspire to "see the *Thing Itself* . . . the quintessence revealed direct without the fog of impressionism."[2] Weston's photographs possess an enigmatic, glossy, black-and-white purity that meticulously presents his subject's form, celebrates his camera's mechanical precision and optical clarity, and simultaneously testifies to the artist's own poetic sensitivity and visual acuity. Crisp and unsentimental, Weston's cemetery images were created with his careful composition, his eye for detail, and his confidence in leading his own private tour away from the trammeled path of his predecessors.

St. Bernard Cemetery, New Orleans. Edward Weston, 1941
New Orleans Museum of Art: Gift of Mr. and Mrs. Arthur Q. Davis. Acc. no. 82.126.1

If Weston's approach was sober and agnostic, Clarence John Laughlin saw New Orleans's cemeteries as playgrounds and backdrops for his surrealist sensibility. Having grown up in southern Louisiana, Laughlin had certainly had countless opportunities to observe how funerals, mourners, tourists, and light infiltrated the gloomy corridors of its burial grounds. There, and also in and around crumbling and abandoned plantation homes—and probably just about anywhere else he chose to look—Laughlin found suitable inspiration for his metaphysical musings, which he shared in writing and through his mysterious photographs. Not simply relying on the camera's ability to find telltale signs of mortality and decay amidst the ruins, Laughlin sometimes orchestrated gothic tales and tableaus for his lens. In these cemetery views, shrouded figures lurk in the shadows, and stone statues seem only temporarily still. Looking at these pictures makes one realize that there can be more to a photograph than what meets the eye. Laughlin's goal was to "subtly penetrate beyond the tough outer skin of appearances, and give us a reality which is not only complexly sweetened or embittered by the perceiving mind, but more extensive in time than the reality which is immediately apprehensible."[3] Laughlin showed us that despite our inclination to think of photographs as history, fantasy is but a simple double-exposure away.

Created with no special equipment (a medium-format camera and sometimes a well-positioned flash), Greiner's photographs, like Edward Weston's, are built with a trust in the medium, careful composition, and an eye for detail. But unlike Weston's, which are reductive, cool, and systematic, Greiner's images evidence a delight for the instantaneous manner with which a camera can record days, months, even years of disorder. There are also significant similarities and differences between Laughlin's and Greiner's cemetery photographs. Like Laughlin's, Greiner's aspire to transcend documentation; they are not just about the decisive instant when the camera made its record, but also about the story that the camera missed. But where

Solitude Has a Face. Clarence John Laughlin, 1939
New Orleans Museum of Art: Bequest of Clarence John Laughlin. Acc. no. 85.118.11

Laughlin sometimes made up the narrative content of his still pictures by adding actors, inserting props, or attaching text, Greiner finds his short stories in nonfictional clues. His pictures are not just about graves, but also about the lives and values of the people who inhabit or visit them. In Greiner's photographs truth is indeed stranger than fiction.

So William Greiner was not the first, nor will he be the last, photographer to explore the cemeteries of New Orleans and southern Louisiana. He knew this well when he made his first exposures in their confines back in 1989. In fact, as a serious student of art history and photography (he received his B.F.A. from Tufts University/School of the Museum of Fine Arts in 1982), he was well acquainted with the efforts of Weston and Laughlin. And having been born and raised in New Orleans, he was also well aware that redundant images of the region's cemeteries were as common as red beans and rice. Greiner's decision to start making the photographs that would coalesce into *The Reposed* was really triply brave: first, he must not have feared ghosts; second he had to watch his back (cemetery tourists in New Orleans have been easy marks for local nefarious types); and third, he was taking on the challenge of photographing the cemeteries knowing how many photographers had haunted the territory before. Greiner has not yet been spooked or mugged, and he has created a series of photographs that looks like no other.

Unlike most of his cemetery-visiting artistic predecessors, and unlike most photographic artists in general, Greiner works in color. The reasons for the preponderance of black-and-white photography in galleries and museums are numerous, but they include the artists' desire to distinguish their work from amateurs' color snapshots, and the ease, low cost, and hands-on involvement of the artist in black-and-white versus color processing. But the reason so many artistic photographs of cemeteries are rendered in black-and-white might be more abstract. In our culture and in our language the word *colorful* is synonymous with "lively" or "animated," whereas gray symbolizes things dull and dreary. White is purity and light, and black is night, death, the color of mourning—the color of our clothes at a funeral. Color photogra-

phy would seem to be the way to go in documenting something cheery like a birthday party or a playground. Black-and-white photography, contributing a monochromatic affirmation of solemnity, is normally the logical choice for sepulchral subject matter.

William Greiner's photographs are thus a colorful respite from the gray conventions of graveyard photography. In these pictures grass is green, not gray, earth is brown, not black, sky is blue, not white, and the flowers, signs, and totems that decorate crypts and plots confer the rest of the color spectrum. However, to talk about color in these photographs as a mere list of adjectives is to sell the pictures short. Some of these photos are about color as surely as they are about cemeteries. Some focus on individual colors such as green or blue, many are about tonal contrasts, and all were made by an artist who is investigating the elemental and expressive potential of chromatics with the same diligence as a Fauvist painter.

Greiner talks openly about the influence of William Eggleston's work on his artistic development. *William Eggleston's Guide,* an exhibition and catalog of the artist's quixotic color photographs presented by New York's Museum of Modern Art in 1976, is often cited as the occasion when unorthodox, color-conscious images first assumed the status of high art. Greiner relates that the *Guide,* along with regular trips to MOMA to see Eggleston's *Red Room* photograph, steered him away from his original career as a sports photojournalist and toward a pursuit of a more personal vision.

Greiner's photographs are also distinct from typical local cemetery images in a less colorful, yet equally significant, way. He takes most of his pictures not in the antique and well-attended cemeteries found on the fringes of the French Quarter or in the Garden District of New Orleans, but in less grandiose and conspicuous burial grounds. Located in transitional spaces between the town and the country, or where old roads lead to new real estate developments, they exist as geographic testimony to our comprehension of the cemetery as the transitional space between our struggle in the earthly realm and the paradise in which we hope to participate. Greiner works in places that are not usually inspected by camera-toting tourists on special excursions but might be glimpsed by thousands of commuters driving by every day. His images disclose, here between the sacred and the suburban, a curious border that you might find for yourself, if you would just pull over, or at least slow down. Greiner's camera reveals a demarcation of hallowed ground that is often as passable as a simple chain-link fence. In these photographs there is no great divide; streetlamps and telephone wires intrude into the heavens, supermarkets and mausoleums share parking lots, and religious and secular symbols vie for attention.

These clues to the discordant harmony between the suburban and spiritual realms lead to many of the individual grave sites that capture the photographer's attention. Here where we expect to find solemn stones, Greiner points to a new visual lexicon of mourning. Where we normally find graves marked only by granite or marble (taken from the ground to which our bodies will return), we suddenly encounter other memorial objects that are more colorful, less massive, but probably as durable; they are made out of plastic. Plastic dolls, polyester ribbons, Styrofoam letters, and brilliant bouquets of plastic flowers adorn these graves and fill these photos. Man-made and formulated to be resilient to the elements and to the swift course of biological decay, these synthetic artifacts seem out of place in these sepulchral settings. Like a bright polka-dotted tie with a gray business suit, they appear outside the boundaries of cautious decorum with which we expect a grave to be accessorized. They also seem cheap. They mark not the decaying bodies of aristocrats, celebrities, and politicians, but those of folks who were less monetarily successful in life. A number of Greiner's pictures were taken in New Orleans's Holt Cemetery, a potter's field where the plots are not owned, but burial rights are conferred for $150. That fee also buys a responsibility to mark the grave

and to maintain it. The families of the dear departed at places like Holt Cemetery construct their own methods of identifying the grave, and their own landscape and maintenance practices using whatever materials they can find or afford. Sometimes with surprising results. Greiner's photographs offer colorful proof of something that we probably suspected but never minded—that different amounts of money create different ways of commemorating death. But where should class consciousness, empathy, and aesthetic appreciation intersect? Do Greiner's photographs strike you as the work of a sardonic tour guide? A compassionate missionary? A dedicated anthropologist? Or are they just nice to look at? In the end (which lurks in all these photos, and waits for us all), death transcends categorization.

Significantly, not Weston, nor Laughlin, nor William Greiner, nor most photographers who enter cemeteries in search of art feature in their photographs the graves of people they personally knew and loved. Perhaps the lack of a blood connection between the photographer and the entombed (like the camera that subtly segregates the photographer from the subject) creates a necessary sense of detachment that allows him or her to search for less personal, yet equally significant, material. Or perhaps it's because, just like the rest of us, photographers use a different sort of image to meditate over loss.

The photograph has supplanted the grave marker, the lock of hair, the painted portrait, the written tribute, and the spoken word as the most common vehicle for the contemplation of the dear departed. The tombstone, as terrestrial marker for the site of the remains, must not move and thus tends to be massive, or at least stuck into the ground as deep as the clay will allow. The lock of hair contains authenticity (and what modern science refers to as the genetic code). The painted portrait is normally an idealization and has the dimension and *gravitas* to fill a prominent space on a prominent wall. The written tribute has a flavor of deliberation, whether it is as short as a few lines of poetry or as long as a novel. And the spoken word by way of reminiscence often resonates with personal and anecdotal familiarity. But it is the photographs of our lost loved ones, flat and fragile, silent and small, and produced in fleeting fractions of a second, that best seem to capture their essence and their mortality. Such photographs are documentation of the past, evidence of ancestry, and proof for posterity. Photographs outlast us, living in albums, shoeboxes, and wallets long after we are gone.

Look around; cemeteries (and photographs of cemeteries) are living proof that people are either dying or losing loved ones all the time. Anyone, from the most obstinate atheist to the most devout religious disciple, can visit a cemetery and be moved toward intense reflection. And this is why many photographic artists are drawn to these places like moths to light. You see, although drastically divergent in their methods and targets, good photographers are on the lookout for something more than pretty pictures. They're out there pointing their cameras at things that matter to themselves and to produce images that they hope will matter to other people as well. Cemeteries, filled as they are with people who have used up their time, compel the living to try to figure out what matters, while there is still some time left.

Death has always been the motivator behind the human search for meaning in life. Only recently—for less than two centuries—has photography proved capable of providing some answers. William Greiner's photographs are about death, but not with the unflinching stare with which the camera can record the snuffing of life. And these photographs are about death, but not how explicitly a picture so perfectly renders the stillness of a corpse. Not a soul appears in these images, but they are haunted nonetheless: by the skeletons of flowers, by chipped statuettes, by faded pictures, and by overgrown grass; by the tangible evidence of the passing visits of those who have come to bury or remember their dear departed; by passing clouds, and by the passage of time.

Look at these pictures and imagine the photographer walking through deserted cemeteries. Think of the wind and the trees, and the sun in his eyes. And recognize that these photographs are memorials of memorials. In the end, it doesn't matter if the flowers are real or plastic, the crucifix marble or wood. It is the gesture that counts, and there are many ways of showing that you care, including taking a picture.

1. This point is made and thoroughly explicated by Peggy McDowell in her chapter, "Influences on Nineteenth-Century Funerary Architecture," in *New Orleans Architecture, Volume III: The Cemeteries* (New Orleans: Pelican, 1994).

2. Edward Weston, *The Daybooks of Edward Weston,* ed. Nancy Newhall (New York: Horizon Press, 1961), 154.

3. Clarence John Laughlin, *Ghosts along the Mississippi* (New York: Bonanza Books, 1961), Prologue.

The Reposed

1.   *Notice Sign,* New Orleans, 1994

3. *1960,* Harvey, 1989

4. *Pink Oval*, Baton Rouge, 1992

5.   *Portrait in Purple,* New Orleans, 1990

6. *Pink Bicycle,* New Orleans, 1993

8. *Ceramic Fish*, Bedico, 1993

9.   *Floral on Fence,* Bogalusa, 1996

10. *Fish on Canvas,* New Orleans, 1992

11. *Shadow on Fence*, New Orleans, 1995

12.   *Two Angels,* Slidell, 1989

13.   *Red Clay and Wreath*, Kentwood, 1990

14. *Red X*, New Orleans, 1995

15.   *Photo Copy Portrait,* New Orleans, 1989

17.   *Broken Heart,* New Orleans, 1990

18.   *Man*, Ponchatoula, 1993

22. *Statue and Clouds,* New Orleans, 1995

23.   *White Wall*, New Orleans, 1989

25.   *Tentacle Vein*, New Orleans, 1995

26.   *Cast Iron Tomb,* New Orleans, 1993

27. *Coffee Can Wreath*, New Orleans, 1989

28.   *Brown Baby without Arms,* New Orleans, 1993

29.   *Brown Bear,* Robert, 1992

30.   *Decayed Wreath*, Larose, 1993

31.   *White Box,* Raceland, 1990

32.   *Car,* New Orleans, 1995

34.   *Storm Front,* New Orleans, 1995

35.   *Green Cross in Foliage,* New Orleans, 1989

36.   *Sewing Machine Picture*, Hammond, 1993

37. *Arch of White Roses,* New Orleans, 1989

38.   *White Bird on Red Wreath,* Pearl River, 1992

39.   *Hands in Prayer,* New Orleans, 1992

40.   *Leafless Trees,* New Orleans, 1991

42. *Elk Statue and Trees,* New Orleans, 1998

44.   *Harley-Davidson Model,* Abita Springs, 1992

45. *Bingo Board*, Luling, 1990

46.   *Plastic Flowers in Bag*, Raceland, 1990

48.   *White Cross*, New Orleans, 1995

49. *In Memory of Our,* New Orleans, 1995

50.   *Ceramic Mary and Jesus,* Cut Off, 1991

51.   *Silver Tomb,* Amite, 1990

52. *Framed Jesus,* New Orleans, 1993

53. *Holy Bible*, Kentwood,

54.   *Angel Ornament,* Denham Springs, 1993

55. *Tilted Wreath Stand,* New Orleans, 1990

56.   *Bird on Blue Wreath,* Bush, 1989

57.   *Blue Guitar,* Des Allemands, 1990

58. *Blue Heart,* Houma, 1989

59.   *Blue Burial Stand*, Des Allemands, 1993

60.   *J*, New Orleans, 1993

61.   *Two Wreath Stands,* LaPlace, 1989

62.　*For Info. Mural,* Metairie, 1989

ACKNOWLEDGMENTS

Where I have found inspiration in the resting places of those who have gone but are not forgotten, thank you to all of their families, friends, and loved ones.

To all of those who have taught, helped, encouraged, advised, guided, and supported me to the completion of this work, thank you—to Erby Aucoin, Ken Barnes, Nancy Barrett, Sandra Russell Clark, Gene Daymude, Jim Dow, William Eggleston, Roger Green, my bride Stephanie, my parents Joe and Shirley Greiner, Leah Bell Kross, John Lawrence, Susan Lipper, Tommy McDonnell, A. J. Meek, John Ramsey Miller, Richard Misrach, Richard Newman, Marguerite Oestreicher, Roger Ogden, Gordon Parks, John Szarkowski, Lew Thomas, and Bill Zeeble.

For the beautiful and insightful words, I would like to thank Thomas Lynch and Steven Maklansky. To my printer at Colour Spectrum Labs, Andy Lipps and company, without whom there would be nothing to hang on the wall.

I am grateful to everyone at Louisiana State University Press for their hard work and efforts in creating this book.

William K. Greiner